TEAM SPIRIT ®
SMART BOOKS FOR YOUNG FANS

THE HOUSTON ASTROS

BY
MARK STEWART

New Hanover County Public Library
201 Chestnut Street
Wilmington, North Carolina 28401

NORWOOD HOUSE PRESS
CHICAGO, ILLINOIS

Norwood House Press
P.O. Box 316598
Chicago, Illinois 60631

For information regarding Norwood House Press, please visit our website at:
www.norwoodhousepress.com or call 866-565-2900.

All photos courtesy of Getty Images except the following:
Pepsi Bottling Group (7),
Black Book Partners Archives (8, 22, 23, 34 bottom right, 39, 40, 42 bottom left, 43 bottom left & right),
SportsChrome (9, 10, 11, 14, 21, 35 top left & right),
Topps, Inc. (15, 20, 24, 34 top, 36, 37 both, 38, 41, 42 top left, 43 top, 45), Author's Collection (25, 33),
Houston Sports Association, Inc. (34 bottom left), Tom DiPace (35 bottom), Matt Richman (48).
Cover Photo: Ronald Martinez/Getty Images

The memorabilia and artifacts pictured in this book are presented for educational and informational purposes,
and come from the collection of the author.

Editor: Mike Kennedy
Designer: Ron Jaffe
Project Management: Black Book Partners, LLC.
Special thanks to Topps, Inc.

Library of Congress Cataloging-in-Publication Data

Stewart, Mark, 1960-
    The Houston Astros / by Mark Stewart.
        p. cm. -- (Team spirit)
    Includes bibliographical references and index.
    Summary: "A Team Spirit Baseball edition featuring the Houston Astros that
chronicles the history and accomplishments of the team. Includes access to
the Team Spirit website, which provides additional information, updates and
photos"--Provided by publisher.
    ISBN 978-1-59953-483-1 (library : alk. paper) -- ISBN 978-1-60357-363-4
(ebook) 1. Houston Astros (Baseball team)--History--Juvenile literature.
I. Title.
    GV875.H64S74 2012
    796.357'64097641411--dc23
                                                2011047960

Manufactured in the United States of America in North Mankato, Minnesota.
196N—012012

COVER PHOTO: The Astros start a wild celebration after their 2005 league championship.

TABLE OF CONTENTS

ABOUT OUR GLOSSARY

In this book, there may be several words that you are reading for the first time. Some are sports words, some are new vocabulary words, and some are familiar words that are used in an unusual way. All of these words are defined on page 46. Throughout the book, sports words appear in **bold type**. Regular vocabulary words appear in ***bold italic type***.

MEET THE ASTROS

The city of Houston, Texas has grown faster and gone through more changes than almost any other place in America. Every year, people from all over the world move there for the warm weather and the business opportunities. What they all have in common is their baseball team, the Astros. You can't call yourself a "Houstonian" unless you call yourself an Astros fan.

The Astros celebrated their 50th anniversary in 2011. They did not win a championship in their first half-century, though it was never for a lack of trying. No team works harder to put good players on the field, and no team has players that love baseball more than the Astros.

This book tells the story of the Astros. Like the city of Houston itself, the team has had many exciting moments to go with a few ups and downs. Perhaps that is why, win or lose, Astros fans always believe a championship is just a year away.

Houston fans and players celebrate Craig Biggio's 3,000th hit. Biggio was a lifelong Astro, playing for the team from 1988 to 2007.

GLORY DAYS

The 1962 season was an exciting one for baseball fans. The **National League (NL)** added two new teams. The Mets played their first season in New York, and a team called the Colt .45s took the field in Houston. A Colt .45 was a powerful pistol used in the Old West. Houston fans simply called their team the Colts.

The Colts gave many young players a chance to prove themselves, which was fun for the fans. But the team lost more often than it won,

which was not nearly as much fun. The fans hoped Houston's luck would change in 1965, when the club moved into a fabulous new indoor ballpark called the Astrodome. That year the team also changed its name to Astros.

Batted balls did not travel far in the Astrodome. That put greater importance on pitching and defense for Houston. The Astros realized this and signed a number of hard-throwing pitchers, including Larry Dierker, Don Wilson, and J.R. Richard. Dierker was the first Astro to win 20 games in a season. Wilson threw two **no-hitters** and once struck out 18 batters in a game. Richard was the first right-handed pitcher in NL history with more than 300 strikeouts in a season.

Finding batters who could do well in the Astrodome was a challenge. During the 1960s and 1970s, the team had a number of talented hitters, including Rusty Staub, Joe Morgan, Jim Wynn, Doug Rader, Cesar Cedeno, Bob Watson, Lee May, Enos Cabell, Jose Cruz, and Terry Puhl. But it just wasn't enough. Houston had a winning record only twice in its first 17 seasons!

During the 1980s, the Astros finally turned things around. They had a winning record almost every year of the *decade*. Houston was led by great starting pitchers such as Nolan Ryan, Joe Niekro,

LEFT: The Astrodome is full for Opening Day in 1965.
ABOVE: Rusty Staub was one of the Astros' early heroes.

Mike Scott, Bob Knepper, and Jim Deshaies. Reliever Dave Smith was the best pitcher in a very good **bullpen**.

In 1980, the Astros won the **NL West** for the first time. Unfortunately, they lost an exciting battle against the Philadelphia Phillies in the **National League Championship Series (NLCS)**. Houston returned to the **playoffs** in 1986 with help from slugger Glenn Davis and base-stealers Bill Doran, Billy Hatcher, and Kevin Bass. Again the Astros lost in the NLCS, this time to the Mets. In both

series, Houston came very close to winning its first **pennant**, only to watch its opponents celebrating after the final out.

During the 1990s, the Astros were led by the "Killer Bs"—Jeff Bagwell and Craig Biggio. Bagwell was one of the game's best power hitters, and Biggio was an expert at getting on base and scoring runs. After relief pitcher Billy Wagner became Houston's main relief pitcher in 1997, the team won four **NL Central** crowns in five seasons. Each

LEFT: For 20 years, Craig Biggio was the man who made the Astros go.
ABOVE: Jeff Bagwell watches a line drive head toward the outfield.

time, however, the Astros lost in the playoffs. The fans were beginning to wonder if they would ever watch them play in a **World Series**.

In 2004, the Houston lineup featured two more Killer Bs—sluggers Lance Berkman and Carlos Beltran. The team also relied on two overpowering pitchers, Roy Oswalt and Brad Lidge. This group led the Astros to the NL **Wild Card**, and then a victory over the Atlanta Braves in the playoffs. It was the first time the team had ever won a *postseason* series.

In 2005, the Astros captured the Wild Card again. This time there was no stopping Houston in its quest to reach the World Series. The Astros raced through the playoffs and won their first pennant.

In the years that followed, age and injuries kept the Astros from returning to the playoffs. Talented players such as Hunter Pence and Michael Bourn were fun to watch, but they could not carry the team by themselves. Eventually, Houston traded Pence and Bourn, plus Oswalt, Berkman, and Lidge. The team looked to a new group of exciting young players, including Bud Norris, Jordan Lyles, J.D. Martinez, and Jose Altuve.

The Astros hoped that these players would lead the team into a new era—an era that included Houston joining the **American League (AL)**. After the 2011 season, the Astros announced that they had agreed to switch from the NL Central to the **AL West**. That gave the Astros a new rival in the Texas Rangers and set the stage for more exciting Houston victories.

LEFT: Roy Oswalt   **ABOVE**: Lance Berkman

HOME TURF

From 1965 to 1999, the Astros played in the Astrodome. It was the world's first modern indoor baseball stadium. The Astrodome's *translucent* roof made it difficult for fielders to see fly balls, so the ceiling panels were painted a dark color. Unfortunately, this prevented sunlight from reaching the field, and all the grass died. The Astros solved this problem in 1966 by installing a playing surface made of soft plastic called Astroturf.

In 2000, the Astros opened a new ballpark. The stadium has a *retractable* roof and a glass wall that gives fans a view of the Houston skyline. Houston's stadium was built on a site where a train station called Union Station used to be located. As a reminder of the city's proud past, a real train sits on a track atop the left field wall. Fans cheer whenever it runs.

BY THE NUMBERS

- The Astros' stadium has 40,950 seats.
- The distance from home plate to the left field foul pole is 315 feet.
- The distance from home plate to the center field fence is 426 feet.
- The distance from home plate to the right field foul pole is 326 feet.

Downtown Houston can be seen beyond the outfield fence at the Astros' stadium.

DRESSED FOR SUCCESS

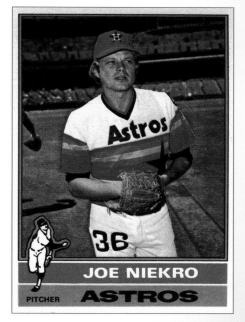

Houston fans have seen some of baseball's most unusual uniforms. From 1962 to 1964, the team's home jersey featured a pistol with smoke rising from its barrel, which formed the *C* in Colts. When the team became the Astros, the gun was replaced with a shooting star. An *H* was combined with the Star of Texas on the front of the team's cap. In 1975, Houston unveiled a red, orange, and yellow sunset design. The players wore their numbers on their pants!

Today, the Astros wear a much less colorful uniform. It uses different combinations of brick red, black, and a grayish color called "sand." For home games, the team often plays in a uniform with ***pinstripes***. Houston's cap features a stylish star.

JOE NIEKRO
PITCHER ASTROS

LEFT: Carlos Lee takes a swing in the team's 2011 road jersey.
ABOVE: Joe Niekro's trading card shows the colorful Houston uniform from the mid-1970s.

WE WON!

In their first three trips to the National League Championship Series, the Astros seemed to be just a few good plays away from winning the pennant. Each time—in 1980, 1986, and 2004—they fell just short. As the 2005 season began, it looked like the Astros would not even make the playoffs. On May 24, Houston's record was 15–30. It had been more than 90 years since a team that was 15 games under .500 had reached the postseason.

From that day forward, the Astros decided they would make a little history. They won 74 games the rest of the way to win the NL Wild Card. Houston was led by a group of young stars, including Morgan Ensberg, Willy Taveras,

Adam Everett, Roy Oswalt, and Brad Lidge. The team also got big contributions from Craig Biggio and Lance Berkman.

The Astros beat the Atlanta Braves in the first round of the playoffs. The final game lasted 18 innings—the longest postseason game in history. The hero was **rookie** Chris Burke, who hit a home run in the bottom of the 18th inning.

Next came the St. Louis Cardinals, who had defeated the Astros in the NLCS the year before. The Cardinals won the opening game 5–3, but Oswalt evened the series by pitching the Astros to a 4–1 win in Game 2. Houston won each of the next two games by a single run. Now they needed just one more victory to reach their first World Series.

The fans in Houston were buzzing as their team built a 4–2 lead in Game 5. In the ninth inning, Lidge needed just three more outs to give Houston the pennant. He retired the first two batters, but the next two reached base. Albert Pujols then took a big swing at the first pitch he saw from Lidge and lined it far over the left field fence. The Cardinals won 5–4.

The Astros put that loss behind them and prepared for Game 6 in St. Louis. Oswalt, who loved to pitch under pressure, shut down the Cardinals all game long. His teammates scored five runs for him, and he allowed only one.

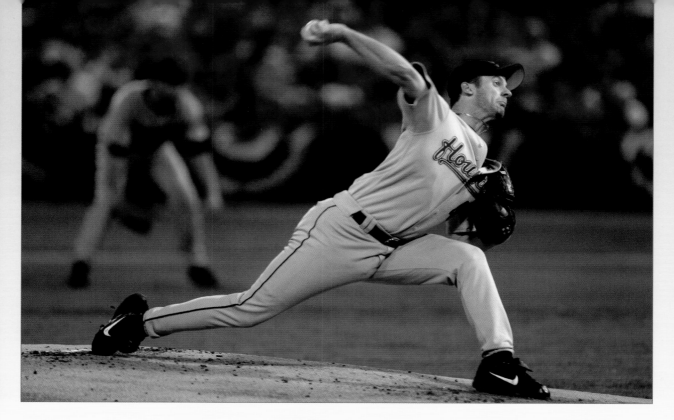

The Astros jumped for joy after the final out. They were finally NL champions. Oswalt was the pitching star of the series, and Biggio was Houston's top hitter.

The only thing that could have made this season sweeter would have been a victory over the Chicago White Sox in the World Series. The two teams played one exciting game after another, but the Astros could not overcome Chicago's great pitching. They lost four close games in a row.

LEFT: Lance Berkman lifts Adam Everett in the air after the final out of the 2005 NLCS.   **ABOVE**: Roy Oswalt held the St. Louis Cardinals to one run on three hits in Game 6.

GO-TO GUYS

To be a true star in baseball, you need more than a quick bat and a strong arm. You have to be a "go-to guy"—someone the manager wants on the pitcher's mound or in the batter's box when it matters most. Fans of the Astros have had a lot to cheer about over the years, including these great stars …

THE PIONEERS

LARRY DIERKER   Pitcher

• BORN: 9/22/1946   • PLAYED FOR TEAM: 1964 TO 1976

Larry Dierker threw his first big-league game on his 18th birthday and struck out the great Willie Mays. He pitched a no-hitter against the Montreal Expos in his last year as an Astro.

JIM WYNN   Outfielder

• BORN: 3/12/1942   • PLAYED FOR TEAM: 1963 TO 1973

Jim Wynn was one of the most powerful sluggers in the league. His nickname was the "Toy Cannon." He hit 37 home runs with 107 **runs batted in (RBIs)** in 1967.

DON WILSON   Pitcher

• BORN: 2/12/1945   • DIED: 1/5/1975   • PLAYED FOR TEAM: 1966 TO 1974

Don Wilson set a team record with 18 strikeouts in a game. Wilson had already pitched two no-hitters for Houston when he died tragically at the age of 29.

CESAR CEDENO   Outfielder

• BORN: 2/25/1951   • PLAYED FOR TEAM: 1970 TO 1981

Cesar Cedeno was baseball's most exciting player in the 1970s. He was a **Gold Glove** center fielder and the first player in history to hit 20 homers and steal 50 bases two seasons in a row.

J.R. RICHARD   Pitcher

• BORN: 3/7/1950   • PLAYED FOR TEAM: 1971 TO 1980

J.R. Richard threw as hard as anyone in baseball. From 1976 to 1979, he won 74 games and struck out more than 1,000 batters. Shortly after starting the **All-Star Game** in 1980, he suffered a ***stroke***, which ended his career.

NOLAN RYAN   Pitcher

• BORN: 1/31/1947   • PLAYED FOR TEAM: 1980 TO 1988

The Astros made headlines when they signed Nolan Ryan in 1980. Houston reached the playoffs for the first time that year, and Ryan pitched a no-hitter the following season.

LEFT: Jim Wynn   **RIGHT**: Nolan Ryan

JEFF BAGWELL   First Baseman

- BORN: 5/27/1968   • PLAYED FOR TEAM: 1991 TO 2005

Few first basemen have ever been as good as Jeff Bagwell. "Bags" was named NL **Most Valuable Player (MVP)** in 1994. In 15 seasons in Houston, he batted .297 and had 449 home runs.

CRAIG BIGGIO   Second Baseman/Catcher/Outfielder

- BORN: 12/14/1965   • PLAYED FOR TEAM: 1988 TO 2007

When baseball fans talk about history's best all-around players, Craig Biggio

is one of the first names they mention. He was an **All-Star** at three positions. In 2007, Biggio became the 27th big leaguer to reach 3,000 hits.

BILLY WAGNER   Relief Pitcher

- BORN: 7/25/1971

- PLAYED FOR TEAM: 1995 TO 2003

Little guys are not supposed to throw hard, but Billy Wagner's pitches often reached 100 miles per hour. In 2003, he had 44 **saves** and struck out 105 batters in 86 innings.

LANCE BERKMAN   First Baseman/Outfielder

- BORN: 2/10/1976
- PLAYED FOR TEAM: 1999 TO 2010

Lance Berkman played college baseball in Houston and was overjoyed when he joined the Astros in 1997. He soon became the greatest **switch-hitter** in team history.

ROY OSWALT   Pitcher

- BORN: 8/29/1977
- PLAYED FOR TEAM: 2001 TO 2010

Roy Oswalt was the second Houston pitcher to win 20 games two years in a row. He was famous for his staring contests with hitters. In 2006, Oswalt had the lowest **earned run average (ERA)** in the league.

CARLOS LEE   Outfielder

- BORN: 6/20/1976   • FIRST YEAR WITH TEAM: 2007

Carlos Lee was a big man who could hit the ball a long way. He had his own cheering section in the left field stands for every home game. Lee had 100 or more RBIs three years in a row for the Astros.

LEFT: Billy Wagner
ABOVE: Lance Berkman

23

CALLING THE SHOTS

Most baseball teams try to keep the same manager for as long as possible. Some, like the Astros, aren't afraid to make a change—especially if they think a new leader will energize the team. For example, Leo Durocher, Terry Collins, and Jimy Williams all had short stays in Houston. They were good managers, but the Astros felt the team would improve with new leadership. Needless to say, the managers who lasted with the Astros all brought something special to the game.

Bill Virdon spent nearly seven years as the Houston manager. Virdon believed in pulling players aside to talk about their mistakes. He did not embarrass them in front of their teammates. Virdon led the Astros to the playoffs in 1980, when he was named Manager of the Year. Houston returned to the playoffs under Virdon in 1981.

Hal Lanier and Larry Dierker also won the Manager of the Year award with the Astros. Lanier lived and breathed baseball. He was the son of a big-league pitcher and grew

up to play for the San Francisco Giants. Lanier was a coach for the St. Louis Cardinals when they won the World Series in 1982 and 1985. The Astros hired him away from their rival in 1986, and he led the team to the playoffs his first year.

Dierker was a popular man in Houston. He was the team's first pitching ace, and later he became a broadcaster for the Astros. In 1997, Dierker moved to the dugout to manage the club. He led the Astros to the playoffs four times in five seasons. During a 1999 game, Dierker collapsed and was rushed to the hospital. He needed an emergency operation on his brain to survive. Dierker recovered and was back in the dugout in a month. He later wrote a book about managing called *This Ain't Brain Surgery.*

Perhaps the best managing change the Astros ever made came in 2004. That year, Houston got off to a slow start. They had a 44–44 record when team owner Drayton McLane decided to hire Phil Garner to shake things up. The Astros finished 48–26 and made it to the playoffs. The following year, Garner managed them to the first pennant in team history.

When a team needs one more win to clinch a championship, it wants its best pitcher on the mound. That was the scene as more than 30,000 fans took their seats in the Astrodome to watch Mike Scott face the San Francisco Giants near the end of the 1986 season. Houston had a big lead in the NL West, so this was not a "must-win" game. But since the team had finished in first place only once before, it was a special occasion.

Scott was having his best season. He had a good fastball as well as a sharp-sinking pitch. When he was able to control both, batters had a hard time telling them apart. Early in the game, Houston fans wondered whether either would be working. Scott hit the first batter with a pitch.

Scott wriggled out of trouble, but walked the first batter in the next inning. Again, he was able to get three outs without allowing a run. That seemed to do the trick. The Giants did not

Jim Deshaies and Kevin Bass carry Mike Scott off the field after his no-hitter in 1986.

get another baserunner until the eighth inning. By then the Astros led 2–0, thanks to a home run by Denny Walling.

In the ninth inning, the fans rose to their feet as Scott returned to the mound. He had not allowed a hit so far. He was three outs from a no-hitter. The cheers grew louder as he struck out the first two Giants. Up to the plate came Will Clark, San Francisco's best hitter. He tapped a grounder to Glenn Davis at first base, who made the out by himself. The crowd roared, Scott raised his arms in victory, and his teammates rushed onto the field and lifted him up on their shoulders.

Scott could hardly catch his breath as he left the field. "I'm numb, I'm tired, but this is fantastic," he shouted when asked how it felt. "Right now, I hope I don't fall down and pass out."

LEGEND HAS IT

JOE
MORGAN
2nd Base

HOUSTON

DID MICKEY MANTLE HIT THE FIRST HOME RUN IN THE ASTRODOME?

LEGEND HAS IT that he did—but this is only partly true. The great New York Yankees' slugger hit a home run against the Astros in the first **preseason** game played in the Astrodome. The day before, however, 21-year-old Joe Morgan hit a home run in an **intrasquad game**. In the team's first NL game Dick Allen of the Philadelphia Phillies blasted the Astrodome's first official home run in a 2–0 win.

ABOVE: Joe Morgan hit a home run in the Astrodome before Mickey Mantle, but it came in an unofficial game.

WHO WAS THE FIRST PLAYER TO WEAR SOCCER CLEATS ON ARTIFICIAL TURF?

LEGEND HAS IT that it was Rusty Staub. In 1965, the Houston outfielder kept slipping on the team's new Astroturf with his metal spikes. "At a certain point, I had enough of that and I started wearing soccer shoes," Staub remembers. Actually, when he batted, Staub would wear a soccer shoe on his front foot and a baseball cleat on his back foot—so he could push off better when he swung. Whenever Staub reached base, he would call timeout, and trade his baseball cleat for a second soccer shoe so he could run the bases without falling.

DID A GAME ONCE GET RAINED OUT IN THE ASTRODOME?

LEGEND HAS IT that one did. On June 15, 1976, the Astros were supposed to play the Pittsburgh Pirates. A rainstorm drenched the Houston area and flooded many of the city's roads. The players arrived early for warm-ups, but as game time neared a couple of things were missing—fans and umpires. The umps finally arrived but, with only a handful of people able to make it to the Astrodome, the game was called off. With no way to leave the Astrodome, the Astros and Pirates moved their food out of the dressing rooms and ate dinner together on the field.

When a team trades for an All-Star in the middle of the season, he's expected to make a big difference in the pennant race. That pressure didn't bother Carlos Beltran one bit. In 2004, he joined the Astros at the end of June. Beltran had already hit 15 home runs for the Kansas City Royals.

After joining the Astros, Beltran slugged 23 more home runs to finish with 38. He became the fourth "Killer B" in the lineup, along with Craig Biggio, Jeff Bagwell, and Lance Berkman. Beltran turned out to be just what the Astros needed. They were stuck in fifth place when he arrived. They finished with 92 victories—enough to make the playoffs as the NL Wild Card.

Against the Atlanta Braves in the playoffs, Beltran came to bat 24 times. He got 10 hits, walked once, and was hit by a pitch. Four of his hits were home runs. Beltran scored nine times and drove in nine runs. He also stole two bases. In the deciding game of the series, Beltran smashed two homers in a 12–3 win.

Next the Astros faced the mighty St. Louis Cardinals in the NLCS. Many fans didn't think Houston had a chance. But Beltran

Carlos Beltran was a hit machine after he joined the Astros in 2004.

was even better against the Cardinals. He hit home runs in each of the first four games. Including his long ball against the Braves, that made homers in five playoff games in a row for Beltran. No player had ever done that before.

The Cardinals finally figured out the way to stop Beltran—they gave him nothing good to hit. In all, he walked eight times in the series. That proved to be the difference. The Cardinals took the NLCS in seven games and went on to win the World Series.

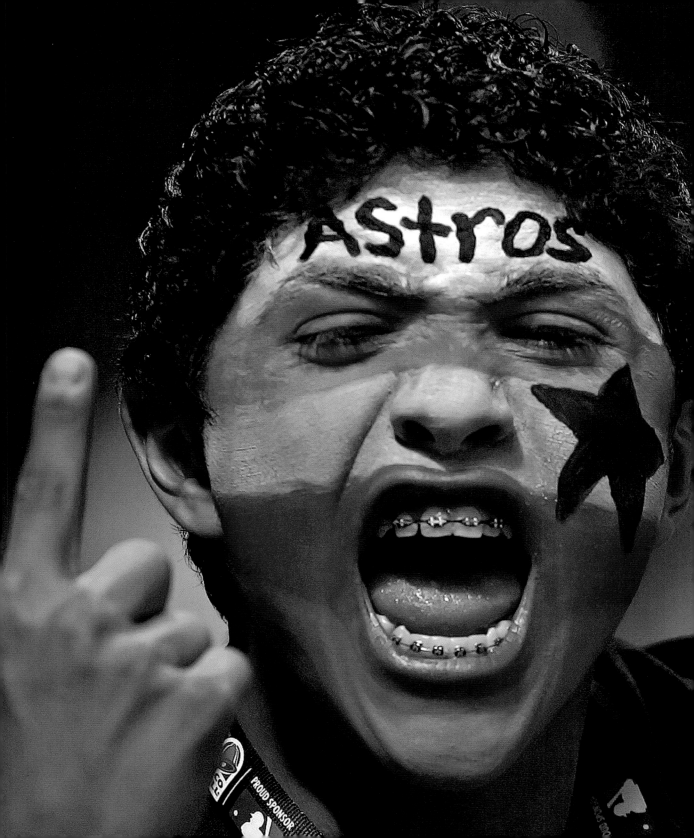

TEAM SPIRIT

A lot of people think that football is king in Texas. That may be true, but the state has been producing great baseball players for more than a century. Fans across Texas celebrated when Houston became a big-league city. Even though the Astros are no longer the only club in the state, a lot of Texans think of the Astros as "their" team.

One of the ways the Astros have rewarded their fans is by building wonderful new stadiums. The Astrodome was considered a marvel in its time. Fans could get away from the Texas heat for a few hours and watch a game in an air-conditioned ballpark. The team's current home is one of the nicest places to enjoy a game. It brings out the best in the Astros and the best in their fans.

LEFT: The Astros have some of the game's most "colorful" fans!
ABOVE: Houston fans could buy this mini pennant during the team's early years.

TIMELINE

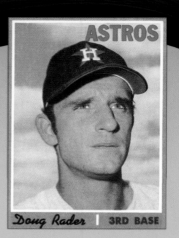

Doug Rader

Doug Rader | 3RD BASE

ASTROS

1962
The Colt .45s win 11–2 in their first game.

1970
Doug Rader is the first Astro to win a Gold Glove.

1972
The Astros have their first winning season.

1965
The team changes its name to Astros and moves into the Astrodome.

1980
The Astros reach the playoffs for the first time.

INSIDE THE ASTRODOME

Eighth Wonder of the World!

260 PAGES OF STORIES, FACTS, FIGURES AND ILLUSTRATIONS ON HOUSTON'S FABULOUS ASTRODOME, THE HOUSTON ASTROS, MAJOR LEAGUE BASEBALL, THE HOUSTON OILERS, THE AFL, THE UNIVERSITY OF HOUSTON COUGARS, EVANGELIST BILLY GRAHAM AND THE HOUSTON LIVESTOCK SHOW AND RODEO.

$1.00

THE MOST COMPLETE SPORTS AND STADIUM BOOK IN THE WORLD!

This guide book was sold for $1 at the Astrodome.

Cesar Cedeno led the 1980 team with 48 stolen bases.

Jeff
Bagwell

Lance
Berkman

2001
Lance Berkman becomes
the first switch-hitter to
hit 50 doubles and 30
homers in the same season.

1994
Jeff Bagwell is
named MVP.

1986
Mike Scott wins the
Cy Young Award.

2005
The Astros win
their first pennant.

2010
Michael Bourn leads
the NL in steals for the
second year in a row.

Michael Bourn
steals a base
against the
Florida Marlins.

FUN FACTS

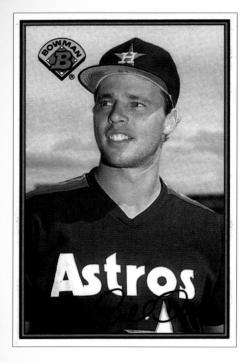

CIRCLING THE BASES

In 2011, Jose Altuve led off a game with an **inside-the-park home run**. The last Astro to do that was Bill Doran, in 1987.

NO DOUBT

Jeff Bagwell's 1994 season was so good that all of the MVP voters made him their number-one choice. It was just the fourth time in NL history that this happened.

BIG SIX

In a 2003 game against the New York Yankees, Roy Oswalt was injured in the second inning. He had yet to give up a hit. Houston had no choice but to go to the bullpen. The Astros used five relief pitchers, who teamed up to finish off the no-hitter.

ABOVE: Bill Doran
TOP RIGHT: Don Wilson   **BOTTOM RIGHT**: Bob Watson

SWEET REVENGE

In April of 1969, the Cincinnati Reds hammered Don Wilson for seven runs in a 14–0 win over the Astros. Nine days later Wilson faced the Reds again—and pitched a no-hitter!

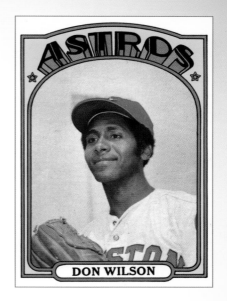

ONE IN A MILLION

On May 4, 1975, Bob Watson scored the millionth run in baseball history.

ARE YOU KIDDING?

In a 1963 game against the New York Mets, the Astros started nine rookies in the field. Manager Harry Craft made history, but it didn't make a difference. The Mets won 10–3.

OH, BROTHER

In 1976, pitcher Joe Niekro hit the only home run of his 22-year career. It came off his brother, Phil, who was pitching for the Atlanta Braves.

"I can't tell you how happy I am. It took us a long time, and we've got five million people in Houston who are very pumped up right now."

▶ *CRAIG BIGGIO*, ON THE FEELING IN HOUSTON AFTER THE ASTROS WON THEIR FIRST PENNANT

"I just prepare myself the best I can and give 100 percent."

▶ *CARLOS LEE*, ON HOW HE GETS READY FOR EACH SEASON

"A good base-stealer should make the whole infield jumpy. Whether you steal or not, you're changing the rhythm of the game."

▶ *JOE MORGAN*, ON THE VALUE OF SPEED ON THE BASEPATHS

ABOVE: Carlos Lee   **RIGHT**: Hunter Pence

"Preparation is the key to success. All the work you put in away from the field will eventually pay off on the field."

► **HUNTER PENCE**, *ON THE VALUE OF HARD WORK*

"One of the beautiful things about baseball is that every once in a while you come into a situation where you want to—and where you have to—reach down and prove something."

► **NOLAN RYAN**, *ON HOW THE SPORT CHALLENGES PLAYERS TO DO THEIR BEST*

"I wanted to play every game of my career in an Astros uniform."

► **LANCE BERKMAN**, *ON HIS LOVE OF HOUSTON AND ITS FANS*

"I've had a great career. I've had a lot of fun. I've met a lot of great people."

► **JEFF BAGWELL**, *ON WHAT HE'LL REMEMBER FROM HIS DAYS IN HOUSTON*

GREAT DEBATES

People who root for the Astros love to compare their favorite moments, teams, and players. Some debates have been going on for years! How would you settle these classic baseball arguments?

JOE MORGAN WAS THE ASTROS' GREATEST SECOND BASEMAN ...

... because he did everything well. Morgan was an excellent fielder, a very fast baserunner, and a smart hitter. When the Astros traded him to the Cincinnati Reds in 1972, it was one of the biggest mistakes the team ever made. Morgan went on to win five Gold Gloves and two MVPs with the Reds. He was elected to the **Hall of Fame** in 1990.

CRAIG BIGGIO BEATS MORGAN ANY DAY ...

... because he was the most *versatile* Astro of them all. Not only was Biggio (LEFT) Houston's best second baseman, he might have been the team's best catcher and best centerfielder, too! He joined the team as a catcher and became an All-Star. Then Biggio moved to second base and won four Gold Gloves. In 2003, the Astros switched Biggio to center field, and he became the best fielder in the league.

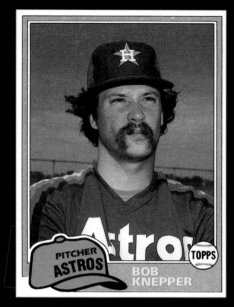

... because they had excellent pitching and tremendous speed. Mike Scott, Nolan Ryan, Bob Knepper (RIGHT), and Jim Deshaies were four of the best starters in baseball in 1986. Dave Smith and Charlie Kerfeld gave the Astros an excellent bullpen. Meanwhile, the Astros drove other pitchers crazy. Bill Doran, Kevin Bass, and Billy Hatcher combined to steal more than 100 bases. No team fought harder from one pitch to the next than the 1986 Astros.

THE 2005 ASTROS WERE THE BETTER TEAM ...

... because they made it to the World Series. Four players had 10 or more steals. Also, the 2005 Astros had good power hitters, including Morgan Ensberg, Lance Berkman, and Jason Lane. As for pitching, they featured Roger Clemens, Andy Pettitte, Roy Oswalt, and Brad Lidge. The 1986 Astros would have been lucky just to get on base against those guys!

FOR THE RECORD

The great Astros teams and players have left their marks on the record books. These are the "best of the best" …

ASTROS AWARD WINNERS

MIKE SCOTT

Mike Scott

WINNER	AWARD	YEAR
Bill Virdon	Manager of the Year	1980
Mike Scott	Cy Young Award	1986
Hal Lanier	Manager of the Year	1986
Larry Dierker	Manager of the Year	1988
Jeff Bagwell	Rookie of the Year*	1991
Jeff Bagwell	Most Valuable Player	1994
Roger Clemens	Cy Young Award	2004
Roy Oswalt	NLCS MVP	2005

* The award given to the league's best first-year player.

Roy Oswalt

Roger Clemens
fires a pitch.

ASTROS ACHIEVEMENTS

ACHIEVEMENT	YEAR
NL West Champions	1980
NL West Second-Half Champions*	1981
NL West Champions	1986
NL Central Champions	1997
NL Central Champions	1998
NL Central Champions	1999
NL Central Champions	2001
NL Wild Card	2004
NL Wild Card	2005
NL Pennant Winner	2005

The 1981 season was played with first-half and second-half division winners.

DARRYL KILE

TOP: Darryl Kile led the 1997 team with 19 wins.
ABOVE: Jose Cruz batted .302 in 1980.
LEFT: Glenn Davis finished second in the 1986 MVP voting.

The history of a baseball team is made up of many smaller stories. These stories take place all over the map—not just in the city a team calls "home." Match the pushpins on these maps to the **TEAM FACTS**, and you will begin to see the story of the Astros unfold!

1 Houston, Texas—*The team has played here since 1962.*

2 New Orleans, Louisiana—*Rusty Staub was born here.*

3 Hollywood, California—*Larry Dierker was born here.*

4 Jefferson City, Tennessee—*Phil Garner was born here.*

5 St. Louis, Missouri—*The Astros won the 2005 pennant here.*

6 Chicago, Illinois—*The Astros played in the 2005 World Series here.*

7 Martins Ferry, Ohio—*Joe Niekro was born here.*

8 Smithtown, New York—*Craig Biggio was born here.*

9 Boston, Massachusetts—*Jeff Bagwell was born here.*

10 Melville, Saskatchewan, Canada—*Terry Puhl was born here.*

11 Santo Domingo, Dominican Republic—*Cesar Cedeno was born here.*

12 Arroyo, Puerto Rico—*Jose Cruz was born here.*

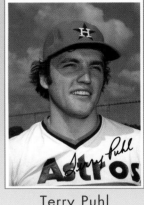

Terry Puhl

45

GLOSSARY

🧠 BASEBALL WORDS
🧠 VOCABULARY WORDS

🧠 **AL WEST**—A group of American League teams that play in the western part of the country.

🧠 **ALL-STAR**—A player who is selected to play in baseball's annual All-Star Game.

🧠 **ALL-STAR GAME**—Baseball's annual game featuring the best players from the American League and National League.

🧠 **AMERICAN LEAGUE (AL)**—One of baseball's two major leagues; the AL began play in 1901.

🧠 **BULLPEN**—The area where a team's relief pitchers warm up. This word also describes the group of relief pitchers in this area.

🧠 **CY YOUNG AWARD**—The award given each year to each league's best pitcher.

🧠 *DECADE*—A period of 10 years; also specific periods, such as the 1950s.

🧠 **EARNED RUN AVERAGE (ERA)**—A statistic that measures how many runs a pitcher gives up for every nine innings he pitches.

🧠 **GOLD GLOVE**—The award given each year to baseball's best fielders.

🧠 **HALL OF FAME**—The museum in Cooperstown, New York, where baseball's greatest players are honored.

🧠 **INSIDE-THE-PARK HOME RUN**—A home run that does not clear the fence.

🧠 **INTRASQUAD GAME**—A game played between players on the same team.

🧠 **MOST VALUABLE PLAYER (MVP)**—The award given each year to each league's top player; an MVP is also selected for the World Series and the All-Star Game.

🧠 **NATIONAL LEAGUE (NL)**—The older of the two major leagues; the NL began play in 1876.

🧠 **NATIONAL LEAGUE CHAMPIONSHIP SERIES (NLCS)**—The playoff series that has decided the National League pennant since 1969.

🧠 **NL CENTRAL**—A group of National League teams that play in the central part of the country.

🧠 **NL WEST**—A group of National League teams that play in the western part of the country.

🧠 **NO-HITTERS**—Games in which a team does not get a hit.

🧠 **PENNANT**—A league championship. The term comes from the triangular flag awarded to each season's champion, beginning in the 1870s.

🧠 *PINSTRIPES*—Thin stripes.

🧠 **PLAYOFFS**—The games played after the regular season to determine which teams will advance to the World Series.

🧠 **POSTSEASON**—The games played after the regular season, including the playoffs and World Series.

🧠 **PRESEASON**—Before the regular season.

🧠 *RETRACTABLE*—Able to be pulled back.

🧠 **ROOKIE**—A player in his first season.

🧠 **RUNS BATTED IN (RBIs)**—A statistic that counts the number of runners a batter drives home.

🧠 **SAVES**—A statistic that counts the number of times a relief pitcher finishes off a close victory for his team.

🧠 *STROKE*—A medical condition caused by a lack of blood flow to the brain.

🧠 **SWITCH-HITTER**—A player who can hit from either side of home plate.

🧠 *TRANSLUCENT*—Allowing light to pass through.

🧠 *VERSATILE*—Able to do many things well.

🧠 **WILD CARD**—A playoff spot reserved for a team that does not win its division, but finishes with a good record.

🧠 **WORLD SERIES**—The world championship series played between the AL and NL pennant winners.

EXTRA INNINGS

TEAM SPIRIT introduces a great way to stay up to date with your team! Visit our **EXTRA INNINGS** link and get connected to the latest and greatest updates. **EXTRA INNINGS** serves as a young reader's ticket to an exclusive web page—with more stories, fun facts, team records, and photos of the Astros. Content is updated during and after each season. The **EXTRA INNINGS** feature also enables readers to send comments and letters to the author! Log onto:

www.norwoodhousepress.com/library.aspx

and click on the tab: **TEAM SPIRIT** to access **EXTRA INNINGS**.

Read all the books in the series to learn more about professional sports. For a complete listing of the baseball, basketball, football, and hockey teams in the **TEAM SPIRIT** series, visit our website at:

www.norwoodhousepress.com/library.aspx

ON THE ROAD

HOUSTON ASTROS
501 Crawford Steeet
Houston, Texas 77002
(713) 259-8000
houston.astros.mlb.com

**NATIONAL BASEBALL
HALL OF FAME AND MUSEUM**
25 Main Street
Cooperstown, New York 13326
(888) 425-5633
www.baseballhalloffame.org

ON THE BOOKSHELF

To learn more about the sport of baseball, look for these books at your library or bookstore:

• Augustyn, Adam (editor). *The Britannica Guide to Baseball*. New York, NY: Rosen Publishing, 2011.

• Dreier, David. *Baseball: How It Works*. North Mankato, MN: Capstone Press, 2010.

• Stewart, Mark. *Ultimate 10: Baseball*. New York, NY: Gareth Stevens Publishing, 2009.

ABOUT THE AUTHOR

MARK STEWART has written more than 50 books on baseball and over 150 sports books for kids. He grew up in New York City during the 1960s rooting for the Yankees and Mets, and was lucky enough to meet players from both teams. Mark comes from a family of writers. His grandfather was Sunday Editor of *The New York Times,* and his mother was Articles Editor of *Ladies' Home Journal* and *McCall's.* Mark has profiled hundreds of athletes over the past 25 years. He has also written several books about his native New York and New Jersey, his home today. Mark is a graduate of Duke University, with a degree in history. He lives and works in a home overlooking Sandy Hook, New Jersey. You can contact Mark through the Norwood House Press website.

ML   3/12